Discover India
State by State

OFF TO GUJARAT

SONIA MEHTA

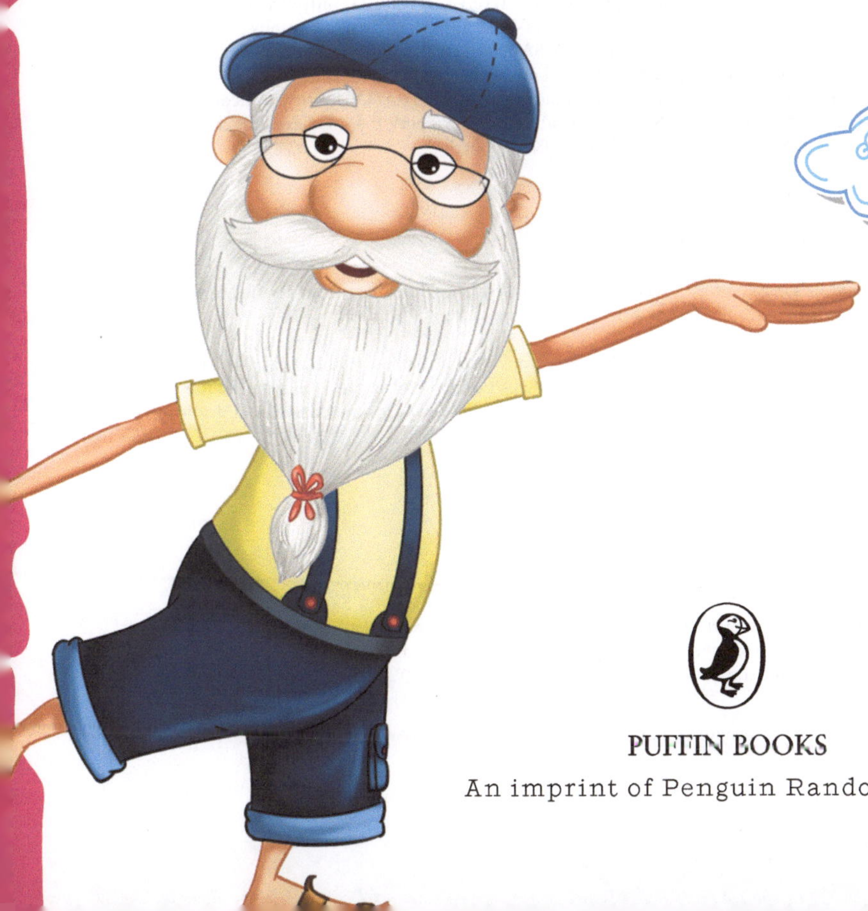

PUFFIN BOOKS

An imprint of Penguin Random House

PUFFIN BOOKS

USA | Canada | UK | Ireland | Australia | New Zealand | India | South Africa | China | Singapore

Puffin Books is part of the Penguin Random House group of companies whose addresses can be found at global.penguinrandomhouse.com

Published by Penguin Random House India Pvt. Ltd
4th Floor, Capital Tower 1, MG Road,
Gurugram 122 002, Haryana, India

Penguin
Random House
India

First published in Puffin Books by Penguin Random House India 2017

Picture Credits

P 12: Rajkot city (© Apoorvjani (Own work) [CC BY 3.0 (http://creativecommons.org/licenses/by/3.0)], via Wikimedia Commons), Dwarka city (O'SHI/Shutterstock.com); P 13: Vadodara city (CamBuff/Shutterstock.com); P 14: Ancient well, Lothal (© Vidishaprakash (Own work) [CC BY-SA 3.0 (http://creativecommons.org/licenses/by-sa/3.0)], via Wikimedia Commons); P 18: Gateway of India (SNEHIT/Shutterstock.com); P 20–21: Traditional house, Bhuj, Gujarat (CRS PHOTO/Shutterstock.com); P 24: Bhavai performance (© Suyash Dwivedi (Own work) [CC BY-SA 4.0 (http://creativecommons.org/licenses/by-sa/4.0)], via Wikimedia Commons); P 26: Bandhani sari (© Sonia Mehta); P 28: Man making manja (pjhpix/Shutterstock.com); P 29: Tarnetar Fair (© Harsh.dattani (Own work) [CC BY-SA 3.0 (http://creativecommons.org/licenses/by-sa/3.0)], via Wikimedia Commons); P 30: Traditional house, Gujarat (Sharad Raval/Shutterstock.com), Traditional Bhunga house (CRS PHOTO/Shutterstock.com); P 31: A traditional Gujarati trade house or haveli (© Namrata Maheshwari); P 32: Ornate door (© Namrata Maheshwari); P 34: Rani ki Vav (Tukaram.Karve/Shutterstock.com); P 37: Cannon at Uparkot Fort (© Bernard Gagnon (Own work) [GFDL (http://www.gnu.org/copyleft/fdl.html) or CC BY-SA 3.0 (http://creativecommons.org/licenses/by-sa/3.0)], via Wikimedia Commons), Jama Masjid, Uparkot (© Bernard Gagnon (Own work) [GFDL (http://www.gnu.org/copyleft/fdl.html) or CC BY-SA 3.0 (http://creativecommons.org/licenses/by-sa/3.0)], via Wikimedia Commons); P 38: Teen Darwaza (© Nichalp [CC BY-SA 2.5 (http://creativecommons.org/licenses/by-sa/2.5)], via Wikimedia Commons), Teen Darwaza (© Iampurav (Own work) [CC BY-SA 3.0 (http://creativecommons.org/licenses/by-sa/3.0)], via Wikimedia Commons); P 39: Ruins at Lothal (© Emmanuel DYAN from Paris, France (Lothal - Gujarat, India) [CC BY 2.0 (http://creativecommons.org/licenses/by/2.0)], via Wikimedia Commons); P 40: Cotton fields, Ahmedabad (CRS PHOTO/Shutterstock.com), Banana plantation (CRS PHOTO/Shutterstock.com); P 43: Man selling handicrafts (Sharad Raval/Shutterstock.com); P 46: Gujarati Daal (© Kekul Sheth), Handvo (©Kekul Sheth); P 47: Daal Dhokli (©Kekul Sheth)

The views and opinions expressed in this book are the author's own and the facts are as reported by her, which have been verified to the extent possible, and the publishers are not in any way liable for the same.

The information in this book is based on research from bonafide sites and published books and is true to the best of the author's knowledge at the time of going to print. The author is not responsible for any further changes or developments occurring post the publication of this book. This series is not a comprehensive representation of the states of India but is intended to give children a flavour of the lifestyles and cultures of different states. All illustrations are artistic representations only.

ISBN 9780143440772

Design and layout by Quadrum Solutions Pvt. Ltd

Printed at Repro India Limited

www.penguin.co.in

This is a legitimate digitally printed version of the book and therefore might not have certain extra finishing on the cover.

Hello Kids!

I'm so happy you are reading this book. India is an incredible country and there are lots of things about it that we never get to hear about.

I discovered India because my father was in the Indian army. He was posted to many places all over India—and we dutifully followed him. Can you imagine that by the time I was in the tenth standard, I had changed nine schools? Of course it was hard making new friends almost every year, but the good part was that I got to live in so many places. Right from Kerala, where I was born, to Kashmir, Jhansi, Shillong, Chandigarh, Goa . . . the list is long.

Every time I go to a new place, I feel amazed at how different each state is from the other—and yet, how similar. Did you know that we can see monuments from the Stone Age right here in India? Or that we have more than twenty official languages, and most Indians know three or four on an average? Or even that some of the world's most amazing scientific marvels were invented in India?

Oh, there are many, many, many fun and fantastic things about the states of India, which we simply must get to know.

So get your backpack ready, get set to meet some new friends and join me on a fun trip as we **DISCOVER INDIA, STATE BY STATE.**

I hope you enjoy reading this book as much as I have enjoyed writing it. I would love to hear from you. So do write to me at sonia.mehta@quadrumltd.com.

Lots of love,
Sonia Aunty

Mishki and Pushka have come to visit Earth from their home planet, Zoomba. They have never seen such an amazing place. Zoomba doesn't have trees and mountains and rivers like Earth does. But the people look exactly the same. When they come to Earth, they meet a sweet old man whom they call Daadu Dolma. Daadu Dolma shows them all the wonderful places in India and tells Mishki and Pushka all about them.

Mishki and Pushka can't believe what they see. They have seen a lot of Earth, but they have never, ever seen a place like India.

They are off to explore India state by state :)

Mishki

Mishki is a curious little girl. She is always asking loads of questions. On her home planet, she is always getting into trouble for poking her nose into things that are not her business.

Pushka

Pushka is Mishki's brother. He **loves adventure**. He is always ready to try a new challenge. Whether it's climbing a mountain, or diving into a cold, cold sea, he is up for it.

Daadu Dolma

Daadu Dolma is a wise old man who has lived on Earth longer than the mountains and seas. No one knows quite how old he is, but he certainly has been around. He knows everything about everything.

Mishki and Pushka have a special treat coming up. They are about to go to Gujarat.

'Daadu Dolma, let's go now,' says Pushka impatiently. 'I have heard so much about Gujarat. I can't wait to see it.'

'Patience,' says Daadu Dolma. 'To really enjoy Gujarat, you must not be in a hurry. It is an amazing state that has produced some of India's most amazing people.'

'Oh wow! And I have heard about their dances too! I want to try them,' says Mishki.

'Well then, what are we waiting for!' says Daadu Dolma. 'Let's go!'

Mishki and Pushka let out a whoop of excitement. They are

OFF TO GUJARAT!!!

A SNEAK PEEK

Land ahoy!

Daadu, I never knew Gujarat was so close to the sea!

It is! It is unique because while it has the sea on one side, it also has India's border with Pakistan on the other!

A FIST INTO THE WATER

Gujarat is shaped like a fist that is jutting out into the Arabian Sea. So it does have a rather long coastline. But it has a lot of land around it too! It has four neighbours—Maharashtra to its south, Rajasthan to its north, Madhya Pradesh to its east and Pakistan to its north-west. No wonder Gujarat has so many different tastes and traditions creeping in.

ON THE MAP

To see exactly where Gujarat is on the map of India, go to http://www.mapsofindia.com/maps/india/india-political-map.htm

WINSOME THREESOME

Gujarat has three main parts—all of them ever so different from the other. Let's see what they are.

Saurashtra: This is an area that is dotted with low hills. A part of this area is called Kathiawad.

Kutch: This is a dry, rocky area.

The mainland: This is a rich, fertile plain, wonderful for farmers.

DESERT OF SALT

The Rann of Kutch is world famous! It is right in the middle of the great Thar Desert. This area is an enormous salt desert and believed to be the largest one of its kind in the world. This is why its sand is white. It has three parts:

Great Rann

Little Rann

Banni Grasslands

Did you know?
Gujarat gets its name from a tribe known as the Gujjars, who lived here centuries ago!

Every winter, hordes of gorgeous pink flamingos form a cloak over the Big Rann of Kutch when they come here to nest. Oh, it's a beautiful sight!

EXTREMELY EXTREME

The climate in most of Gujarat can be called extreme. Do you know why? Because so much of it is desert land. In the summer, the heat turns the whole state into an oven. And in the winter, this area turns into a freezer! But in the middle, there is a comforting monsoon. There is a part of Gujarat that is not arid, and that part has a tropical climate like most of India has.

A temple on Mount Girnar

MOUNTAIN MAJESTY

Gujarat has some amazing mountainous regions. The edges of mountain ranges like the Aravalli, Vindhya, Satpura and Sahyadri give Gujarat a wonderful atmosphere. Some of these ranges have mountain peaks that have become important for both historic and religious reasons, like Mount Girnar.

The Narmada, flowing through Gujarat.

Did you know?
For years, Mahatma Gandhi, the father of our nation, lived in a little hut on the banks of the Sabarmati River. His house, Sabarmati Ashram, is still there.

ROARING RIVERS

There are some magnificent rivers that flow in Gujarat. The Sabarmati, which originates in Rajasthan, is one of Gujarat's largest rivers. The Saraswati, born in a place called Koteshwar, disappears into the salt desert. The Narmada, the longest of them all, starts off in Madhya Pradesh but rushes through Gujarat into the Arabian Sea. Many of these great rivers have tributaries that criss-cross the state.

In desert areas, people have to walk for miles to get water.

In the scorching summer, some of the rivers dry up—especially in the desert region. During this period, a lot of Gujarat is parched.

Pushka has already forgotten what he has learnt. But Mishki remembers. See if you do too. Look for the rivers and mountains of Gujarat hidden in this word search.

WORD SEARCH

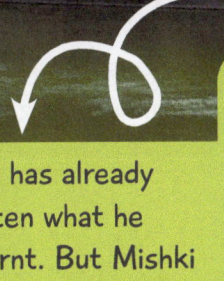

V	I	N	D	H	Y	A	U	I	O
W	S	A	T	P	U	R	A	E	W
D	E	A	R	A	V	A	L	L	I
S	A	H	Y	A	D	R	I	R	Y
C	D	R	G	I	R	N	A	R	G
W	S	A	R	A	S	W	A	T	I
N	J	F	N	A	R	M	A	D	A
S	A	B	A	R	M	A	T	I	B

FOREST FANTASY

Despite a large part of Gujarat being desert land, there are some fantastic forests here! These are mostly in the hilly parts that are towards the south and east of the state. They are tropical deciduous forests, full of teak trees. Other parts have forests that are not evergreen and shed their leaves in March and April. There are parts that have large patches of bamboo growing too!

Asiatic lion

Cheetah

Indian jackal

WILD AND WONDERFUL

You'd never believe that a dry state like Gujarat could have such amazing wildlife. But thanks to its forests and mountains, there is a lot of diversity. The Gir Forest is home to the famous Asiatic lion, as well as smaller animals like blue langurs, gazelles, spotted deer, panthers, cheetahs, jackals, tigers and many more.

Fun Facts!!

State animal:
Asiatic lion

State tree:
Banyan

State flower:
Marigold

State bird:
Great flamingo

BIRDS APLENTY

The thick, lush forests of Dang, which get the most rainfall, have some rare birds like hornbills, barbets, babblers, racket-tailed drongos and minivets. The long coastline breeds other birds like plovers, stints, sandpipers, curlews, lesser flamingos, terns and gulls. And the dry region of Kutch shelters still others like flamingos, grey partridges, larks, white-eared bulbuls and sand-grouses.

Sand-grouse

Flamingo

Crested lark

WHAT'S ODD

There is a word in each row that doesn't belong. Mishki can't seem to find it. Help her circle the word.

Hornbill	**Babbler**	**Bulbul**	**Lion**
Panther	**Elephant**	**Cheetah**	**Tiger**
Aravalli	**Himalaya**	**Satpura**	**Vindhya**
Sabarmati	**Narmada**	**Ganga**	**Saraswati**

??

CITY CITY BANG BANG

Gujarat has some of India's most thriving and vibrant cities. Here are some of them.

This used to be an important city for trade. Now it is well-known for its handicrafts.

BHAVNAGAR

This city used to be the capital of Gujarat.

AHMEDABAD

GANDHINAGAR

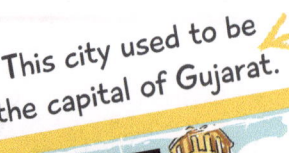

This is the new state capital of Gujarat. It is named after Mahatma Gandhi.

DWARKA

This is Lord Krishna's city. People say Lord Krishna lived here. It is one of India's most important religious places.

RAJKOT

This city has become very important as the administrative headquarters of Gujarat. And its famous pedhas, of course.

This city is very important to the Jains, for it has some of the most important Jain temples.

PALITANA

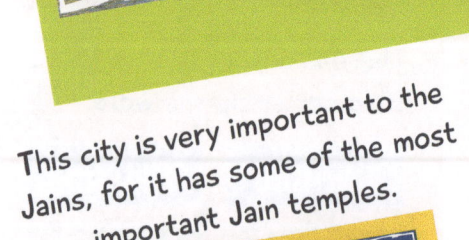

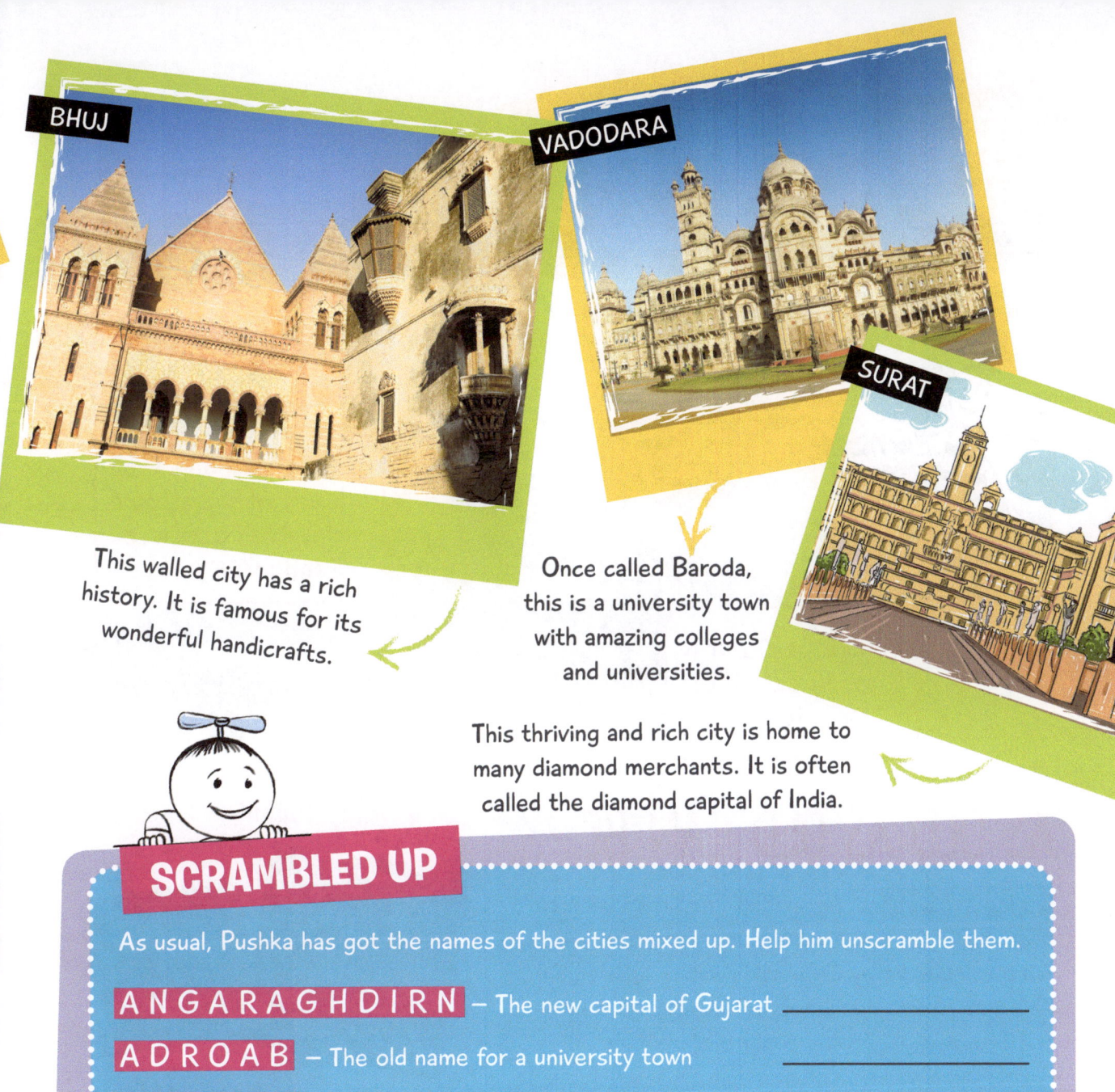

BHUJ

VADODARA

SURAT

This walled city has a rich history. It is famous for its wonderful handicrafts.

Once called Baroda, this is a university town with amazing colleges and universities.

This thriving and rich city is home to many diamond merchants. It is often called the diamond capital of India.

SCRAMBLED UP

As usual, Pushka has got the names of the cities mixed up. Help him unscramble them.

ANGARAGHDIRN — The new capital of Gujarat _____

ADROAB — The old name for a university town _____

AKRAWD — Lord Krishna lived here _____

DABADEMAH — The old capital of Gujarat _____

HUJB — A walled city _____

TARSU — The diamond centre _____

Long, long ago

Oh no, it's not new. Well, the state as we know it is sort of new. But the land of Gujarat and the history of the people who lived here are really VERY old.

Daadu, is Gujarat a really old state? Or is it new?

Ancient well in Lothal, Gujarat

AS OLD AS OLD CAN BE

During excavations, remains of life dating back to over 3500 years ago were found. A part of the famous Indus Valley Civilization was in this region. This means that the history of Gujarat goes back to the Bronze Age. That is super old!

These seals found in Gujarat are thousands of years old.

A CIVILIZATION BEFORE CIVILIZATION

It is believed that explorers came via the sea and occupied a part of Gujarat that already had settlements. For a while, the Harappan Civilization flourished. Historians discovered many items here that indicate that this area was important for trade. After this time, the history of this region becomes a little fuzzy. But then suddenly we see the Mauryan Empire spreading here.

A MAURYA PRESENCE

The great Mauryan king Ashoka ruled over a large part of Gujarat for a while. We know this because there are rock inscriptions in the Girnar Hills that suggest this. But after a while, the Mauryas were defeated by a dynasty called the Sakas or the Scynthians.

King Ashoka of the Mauryan dynasty

Did you know?

Ashoka became a Buddhist when he saw the destruction that wars caused.

MANY KINGS, MANY DYNASTIES

Many different dynasties took over Gujarat, each leaving behind their own mark in the state's religious practices and architecture. Maitraka, Gurjara-Pratihara, Solanki, Vaghela—all these were different Hindu dynasties that came and went, fighting their own wars for control.

Mihir Bhoj was a Gurjara-Pratihara king.

MUSLIM INVASION

The last Hindu dynasty to rule Gujarat was that of the Vaghelas. Alauddin Khilji, who was a fierce Muslim warrior, defeated the last king of the Vaghelas. And with that, Muslim rule in this area began.

A king named Ahmed I, the first independent ruler of Gujarat, established his capital city and named it after himself—AHMEDABAD!

A 200-YEAR RULE

The Mughals, who were conquering area after area across India, soon got their hands on Gujarat. Humayun and then his son Akbar made sure that they got a stronghold on this region. The Mughals ruled over most of India for the next 200 years, until the Marathas, with Shivaji at the helm, overthrew them.

Muslim rulers conquered different parts of India.

16

COLONIAL COUSINS

All this while, different European countries were trying their best to capture ports along the west coast of India. The Dutch, the French, the English and the Portuguese all established a base for themselves along the coast of Gujarat. But eventually, it was the British who proved to be the strongest. They gradually took over all of India. They set up the headquarters of the East India Company in Surat and in Bombay too.

EAST INDIA COMPANY.

Crazy Crossword

Help Mishki and Pushka solve this crossword.

DOWN

1. They pushed the Dutch, the French and Portuguese out and ruled India.

2. Emperor Ashoka's edicts can be seen at this mountain.

3. The diamond capital of Gujarat.

4. A great Maurya king.

5. He named a city after himself.

ACROSS

3. The Maratha king who made the Mughals' lives miserable.

6. An old, old city in the Indus Valley Civilization.

17

A PROVINCE CALLED GUJARAT

All over India, people were fighting and struggling to become independent of the British, who had taken over the country. The British had even pushed out the Portuguese, who were trying to settle in Daman and Diu in Gujarat. The British then called the entire region the Gujarat Province. It was made of many, many smaller princely states, each ruled by a small-time king.

Did you know?
Mahatma Gandhi, who played such an incredibly important role in India's freedom fight, was from Gujarat.

Gandhiji walked across Gujarat during the Dandi March.

INDEPENDENT AT LAST

After a long and aggressive struggle, during which many people from Gujarat played an important role, the British finally left India. Gujarat became a part of Bombay State. A few years later, Saurashtra and Kutch were added on, and in 1960, the state of Bombay was divided into Maharashtra and Gujarat. This was done on the basis of the language spoken by the people in these areas.

THE PARSI CONNECTION

Parsi people are followers of an Iranian prophet called Zoroaster. They are originally from Persia. Centuries ago, because they were not treated very well in their homeland, they left to find a new place where they could live in peace. They landed in Diu, in Gujarat, and were welcomed by the rulers. Slowly they spread to other parts of Gujarat. Today, the Parsis speak Gujarati as their mother tongue.

Women wear saris in the Gujarati style. But they still have their own unique customs.

Zoroaster, the Parsi prophet

There are many famous Parsi people who have done so much for Gujarat and India! Great industrialists like Jamsetji Tata and J. R. D. Tata, scientists like Homi Bhabha and sportsmen like Nari Contractor are some of them.

HIDDEN WORDS

The word SAURASHTRA is a rather long word. Mishki has found many small words hidden in it. How many can you find?

S A U R A S H T R A

_____   _____

_____   _____

_____   _____

_____   _____

Talk time

SPEAKING GUJARATI

The people of Gujarat mainly speak Gujarati. But did you know that there are many types and dialects of Gujarati—some of them closer to other languages from just across Gujarat's border. In the past, there was a common language spoken by the Rajasthani and Gujarati people. Slowly the language evolved. Here are some dialects.

Kathiawadi   Surti
Kharwa   Kutchi

Kem cho, Daadu Dolma?

Where did you learn that? Do you know what it means?

We heard someone talking. But we don't know what it means. Will you please tell us?

How are you? = Kem cho?
I am fine = Hoon maja ma choo
What news? = Soo khabar?

What is your name? = Tamaru naam su che?
Where are you going? = Tamey kyan jao cho?
I don't know = Maney khabar nathi

Bye-bye = Aav jo
How much does it cost? = Ketla paisa laagse?
I am hungry = Maney bhookh lagi che
I am thirsty = Maney taras lagi che

MATCH THE WORDS

Let's see how much you remember. Without looking at the meanings, can you match the English words to their Gujarati translations? Pushka remembered them all!

What news?	I don't know	I am fine	I am thirsty	How are you?	Bye-bye

Aav jo	Maney taras laagi che	Kem cho?	Hoon maja ma choo	Soo khabar?	Maney khabar nathi

21

A peep into their life

Look at how those people are twirling, Daadu! What are they doing?

They are doing a dance called garba. There are many amazing dances that Gujarat is known for. Come, let's see Gujarat's colourful culture.

TWIRL TWIRL TWIRL

Garba is a high energy folk dance. In its original form, women would form a circle with a mud lamp on their heads. The lamp would have holes in it, through which you could see a flame. The women would dance in a circle around an image of Goddess Durga. Now, men and women do this dance during celebrations and during a nine-day festival called Navratri.

HAPPY DANCE

This dance form—called raas—is really very old. As old as Lord Krishna! Men and women form a circle and do this happy dance by tapping two sticks together. These sticks are called dandiyas. During Navratri in some parts of Gujarat, people make concentric circles, and sometimes even a thousand people dance together.

ROUND AND ROUND

This curious dance called hallisaka is performed by women who form a circular chain by holding hands. A man stands in the middle of the circle. He is supposed to be Lord Krishna. The women clap their hands and tap their feet to a beat and build up the tempo.

Did you know?
It is said that Lord Krishna used to do this dance with the local milkmaids.

GETTING EMOTIONAL

There's a really fascinating type of musical theatre performance in Gujarat called Bhavai. 'Bhava' means expressing emotions. The songs and stories are usually about life in the desert or in the countryside. The play goes on all night. The performers use an instrument called a bhungal, which is a long brass wind instrument. Different wandering tribes love to perform this. Sadly, women are not allowed to act. Men play the women's role instead.

RAGAS FROM GUJARAT

There are many ragas that have been composed in Gujarat, and they are even named after tribes of Gujarat. Todi, Bilaval, Sorathi, Ahiri—these are all names of tribes or places in Gujarat, and they're ragas too.

Did you know?

A raga is a musical composition made using only specific notes. This is the basis of Indian classical music.

MASTERS OF INSTRUMENTS

Did you know that many incredible instruments were invented in Gujarat? There are wind instruments like bhungal, turi and pava; there are percussion instruments like manjira and the zanz pot drum; and there are string instruments like ektara, jantar and ravan hattho. All of these are seen in Gujarat's folk music, which is centuries old.

The ravan hattho is a traditional instrument from Gujarat.

WRITER'S BLOCK

Literature has always been very important in Gujarat. Hundreds of years ago, a man called Narsinh Mehta wrote about human values. He is called the father of Gujarati literature. Many centuries later, a man called Premanand introduced a kind of storytelling called Akhyan. Many more writers and poets added their own style.

Narsinh Mehta, the father of Gujarati literature

POEM TIME

Mishki is inspired and wants to write a song about Gujarat. Help her complete the rhymes!

I'm in Gujarat, and this is my chance

I want to sing, I want to _____

Musical instruments make such a lovely sound

They make me want to dance _____

A story in a poem, a story in a song

Come on everyone, let's sing _____

A RIOT OF COLOURS

Say Gujarat and you think of colour. Guess why! Because this state has a long, long tradition of handicrafts. Needlework, dyed fabric, colourful furniture, beadwork . . . Oh, the people of Gujarat are very talented and creative!

TIE-DYE

This is an amazing technique in which a piece of cloth is crumpled and tiny knots are tied all over it with string or rubber bands. The cloth is then dyed in a bright colour. When it dries, the string is removed and lovely patterns emerge. The tie-dye fabric made in Gujarat is bought all over the world; that's how popular it is. This is called bandhani.

PATCHWORK

For centuries, women have been creating brilliant patchwork patterns for quilts, wall hangings and bedspreads. It's a hugely popular craft.

PATOLA PATTERNS

A place called Patan in Gujarat is world-famous for this incredibly beautiful weave. People have been creating these designs on saris for generations.

WOODWORK OF SANKHEDA

There is a place called Sankheda, where for generations, people have been carving the most beautiful details on wood. This wood is used to make furniture, swings and temple doors.

TIE - DYE SHIRT

How about making your own tie-dye T-shirt? Here's what you need:

An old white T-shirt Some rubber bands Coloured fabric dye

Step 1: Scrunch parts of your T-shirt and tie little knots with the rubber bands.

Step 2: Soak the entire T-shirt in the dye.

Step 3: Once the colour has spread over the entire T-shirt, take it out and hang it to dry.

Step 4: Once it's dry, remove the rubber bands.

VOILA! You will have a lovely pattern on your T-shirt.

TIME TO CELEBRATE

There are more than 3500 festivals and fairs that are celebrated all through the year in Gujarat. Whew! That's a lot of celebration! Apart from Diwali, Holi, Eid and other national festivals, there are some that are especially big in Gujarat.

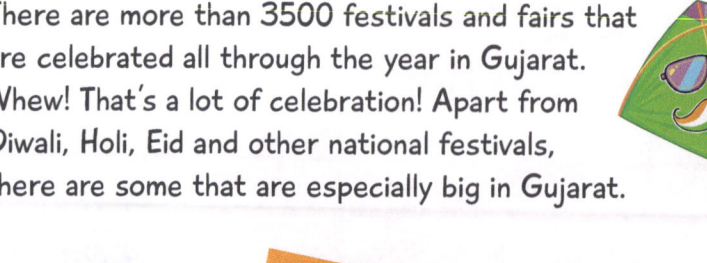

LET'S FLY A KITE

The month of January brings with it strong winds. It is also the month of harvest—and time for the Makar Sankranti festival. In Gujarat, this is celebrated by flying kites. The sky is dotted with hundreds of bright colours, as grown-ups and children collect on the roofs and terraces of their buildings to fly kites.

CIRCLE OF JOY

Navratri is probably the biggest festival. Though it is celebrated in many parts of India, the celebration in Gujarat is the biggest. For nine nights, people get together and pray to Goddess Amba. They do the famous raas and garba dance. People dress up in resplendent traditional costumes and twirl to the sound of drums and music that is played loudly—late into the night. The tenth day is the important day of Dussehra.

FIND-ME-A-BRIDE FAIR

One of Gujarat's most fun fairs, the three-day Tarnetar Fair is held near the Tarnetar Temple. Guess why it takes place. Young tribal men come to find brides. Maidens dress up so they too can find the right match. There are puppet shows, folk music, games, food and loads of fun.

Tarnetar Fair

PUSHKA'S KITE

Which one of these is Pushka's kite? Trace the string and find out!

Bricks and stones

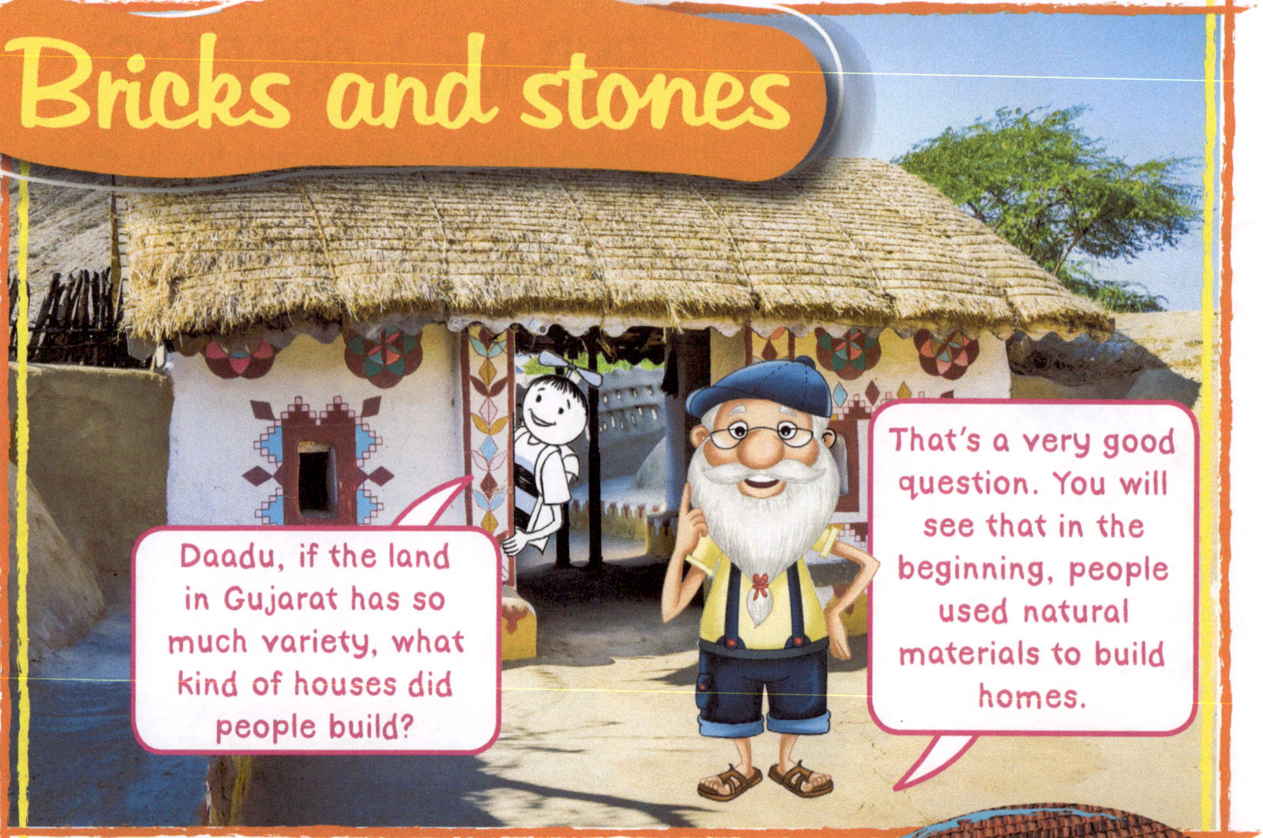

Daadu, if the land in Gujarat has so much variety, what kind of houses did people build?

That's a very good question. You will see that in the beginning, people used natural materials to build homes.

CIRCLE HOUSES

Wall decorated with tiny mirrors.

The land in Kutch is harsh and rocky. So people living here made houses of rocky sand and mud, with thatched roofs. Because everything outside was so dry and dreary, people brightened up the walls with colourful patterns and tiny mirrors. Do you know what's special? These are circular houses! They are called bhungas.

Bhunga houses are very light. This is because there are a lot of earthquakes in this region. In case there's an earthquake and a house comes crashing down, no one gets hurt.

BOHRA HOUSES

Many years ago, a large Muslim community from Gujarat called the Bohras built unique houses called Bohrwads. These people were religious and lived in large joint families. The houses had many rooms. Look at how it was divided.

WOODEN HAVELIS

Emperor Ashoka loved wood carvings. Maybe because of his influence, there are many beautiful homes in this state that are made of wood and have a haveli style. Today, there are many havelis in Gujarat that are considered treasures. They all have a similar structure and look.

1 A terrace called agashi

2 An entrance platform called otla

3 An entrance archway called deli

4 Rooms called ordo

5 A common courtyard called avas

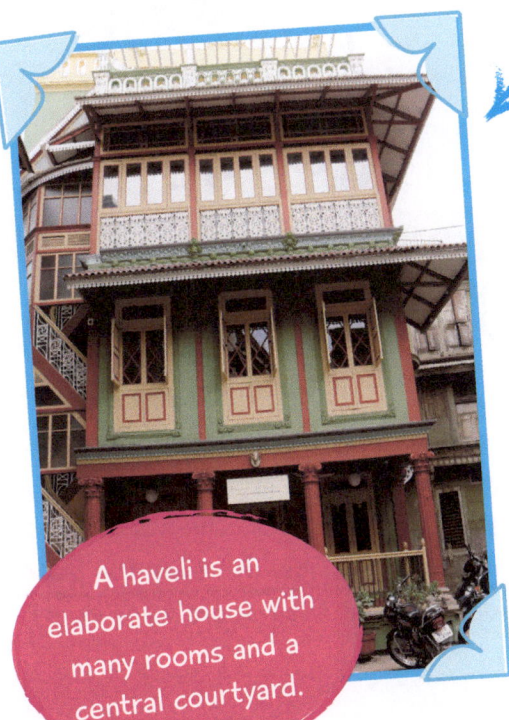

A haveli is an elaborate house with many rooms and a central courtyard.

Word Ladder

H	O	T

(we put tea in this)

(a position for a photograph)

(a tube)

H	O	U	S	E

Can you help Mishki move up the word ladder and change HOUSE to HOT? Change or drop one letter in each word as you climb the ladder. Look at the clues.

'POL' POSITION

The pols of Ahmedabad are fascinating. A pol is a collection of many houses that are built really close together. Some pols even have 3000 houses. These pols have entry gates. The houses are so close to each other that you could actually lean out of your window and shake hands with your neighbour! All houses inside a pol have a specific design. And yes, the courtyard or chowk is a MUST. There are small recesses in the walls, where people keep lamps at night.

Many of the pols have now become leather, brass or cloth markets. Some others are making way for gleaming high-rise buildings too!

DOORS DOORS DOORS

The doors of traditional Gujarati homes were often very detailed and elaborate. Sometimes painted in bright colours, they had brass rings and knobs. The wealthy had more detailed carvings. But even the poor made sure that their doors were lovely.

THE FAMOUS GUJARATI SWING

Traditional Gujarati homes, you will see, almost always have a swing. This is called a hichko. The richer the family, the more elaborate the swing. You would think this was for the kids in the house, right? Oh no! It's often the older family members who sit and swing gently through lazy afternoons and evenings. Must be lovely.

Wow . . . this looks like fun!

A beautifully carved swing used in most Gujarati homes.

People sell these old swings today at an enormous price because they are vintage (which means very old and valuable).

That's ODD

Daadu is giving Pushka a challenge. He has to find one odd word in each of the rows. Can you help?

Swing	Chair	Table	Door
Pol	House	Wall	Apartment
Gate	Window	Arch	Door

Daadu, look! Such interesting buildings.

You can't call them just buildings. They are monuments, built centuries ago. They tell us so much about how life was in Gujarat hundreds of years ago. Let's visit some of them.

QUEEN'S STEPWELL IN PATAN

Imagine having to climb down dozens of steps every time you need water. That's what people had to do hundreds of years ago. The rulers had made this special system called stepwells or vav. This was a well dug deep, close to a water source. People would come here to collect water. The kings would get these built so that people in some of the driest areas had plenty of water. There are many such stepwells in Gujarat, but one which has been declared a UNESCO World Heritage Site is the Rani ki Vav (Queen's Stepwell) in Patan.

WORSHIPPING THE SUN

There was a king called Bhimdev, who was a great worshipper of the Sun god, Suryadev. He ordered this magnificent temple to be built in a place called Modhera in Gujarat. Do you know what's special about this? It is designed in such a way that the sun shines on the image of Suryadev at dawn. It has beautiful pillars on which scenes from the Ramayana and the Mahabharata are carved.

What beautiful stone pillars!

JAIN TEMPLES OF PALITANA

There is a large cluster of close to 900 beautiful Jain temples in a place called Palitana. To reach there, you have to climb nearly 4000 steps. Whew! Over the centuries, different kings who followed Jainism built these beautiful temples. Today, people from all over the world come to pray at these wonderful places of worship.

STEP UP

Pushka is confused. He's been climbing up these steps for hours, but he never seems to go any higher!

This is called an optical illusion. It means that the picture can trick you!

LORD OF THE MOON

There is a beautiful temple called Somnath Temple. It is a Shiva temple. People believe that this was one of the twelve places in India where Lord Shiva appeared in a blaze of light, and a Shiv linga appeared from the ground. There are many legends surrounding this magnificent temple. It has been destroyed again and again by attacking kings, but it's been rebuilt time and again to its wonderful glory.

Did you know? India's first president, Dr Rajendra Prasad, inaugurated the modern temple structure that stands today.

What a beautiful temple!

That is the Somnath Temple. It has an exciting legend behind it.

LEGEND OF SOMNATH

The story goes that the moon once married twenty-seven daughters of a king called Daksha Prajapati. But he loved one daughter much more than the others. The king was upset, and he cursed the moon to lose all his shine. The moon got worried. He prayed long and hard at the Somnath Shiv linga. And that's how he got his shine back.

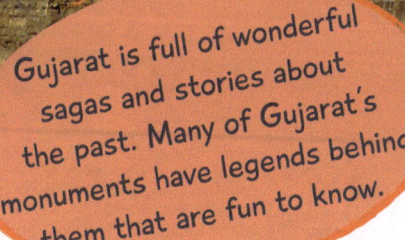

Gujarat is full of wonderful sagas and stories about the past. Many of Gujarat's monuments have legends behind them that are fun to know.

Lord Shiva is worshipped in almost every state.

AKSHARDHAM

One of the largest temples in Gujarat, this modern temple was built just over twenty-five years ago. It is really different because it brings together art, education, architecture and culture. There is a huge idol of Lord Swaminarayana, who is the main deity worshipped here.

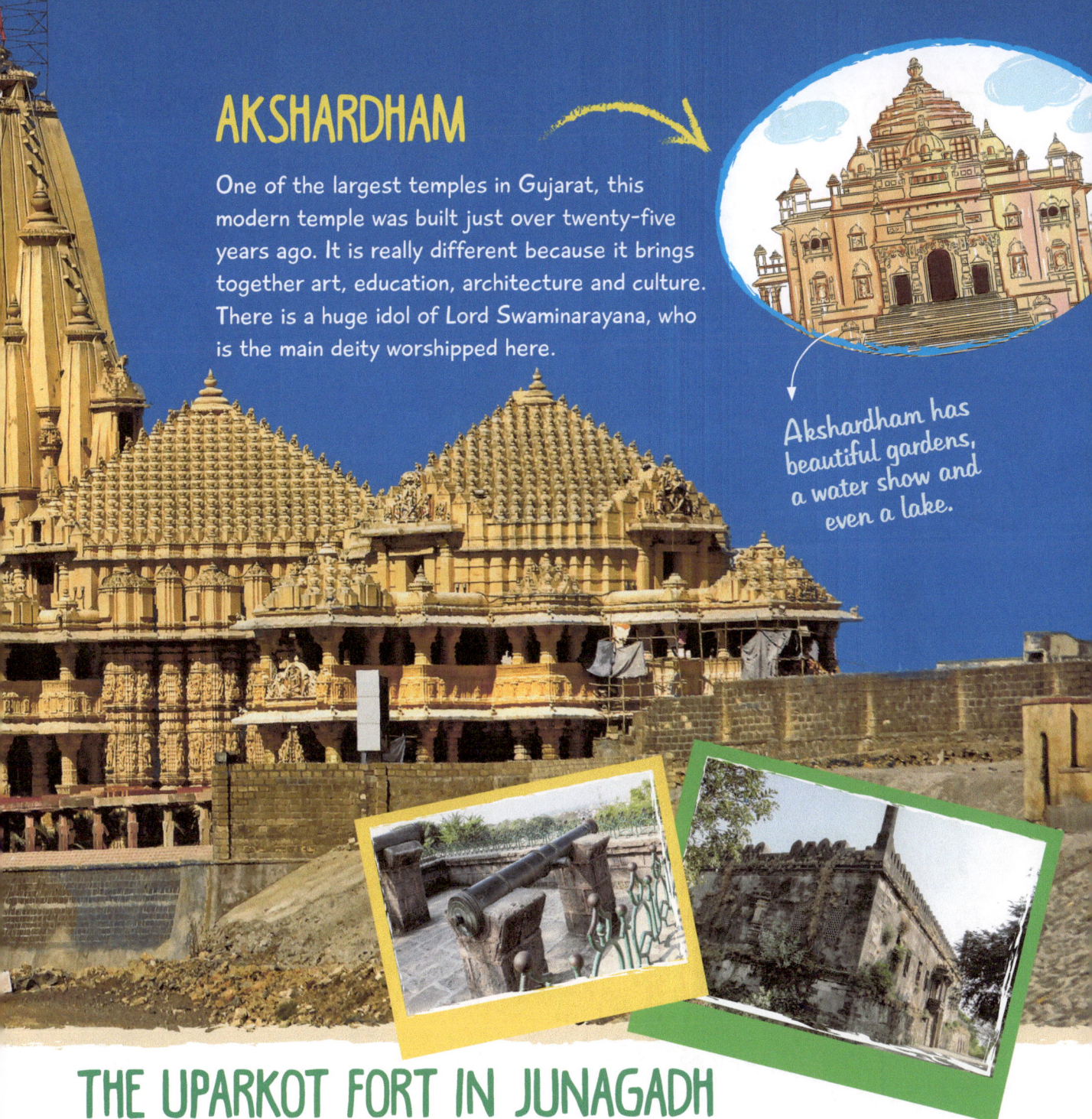

Akshardham has beautiful gardens, a water show and even a lake.

THE UPARKOT FORT IN JUNAGADH

There are many forts in Gujarat. This one is special. It was first built during the Muslim rule, but it has many touches that are Hindu, Buddhist, Jain and British too. In fact, there is even a mosque within the fort, as well as Buddhist caves that are thousands of years old. It also has a large moat that kept enemies at bay.

TEEN DARWAZA

This is one of Ahmedabad's oldest monuments, constructed when the city was built by Ahmed Shah I. It has detailed carvings and was once the entrance to the city. They say that the Mughal emperor Jehangir used to come here with his wife Noor Jehan to see the grand processions that went through these doors.

Minarets that sway when force is applied here

I would love to be on the minaret when it sways.

MINARETS THAT SWAY

This amazing structure is called Jhulta Minar (meaning swaying minaret). It is actually a part of a mosque. They say that when anyone applies force on the uppermost arc, the minaret sways gently.

Ooh, how exciting!

A LOST CITY

In the city of Lothal, very close to Ahmedabad, lie some ruins that were once a part of the Indus Valley Civilization. It is believed that in ancient times, Lothal was a big trading centre of gems, beads and jewellery. People also say that the residents of this city were advanced scientists, who understood astronomy and navigation.

The ancient city of Lothal, which was highly advanced.

WORD GRID

Wow! Mishki and Pushka sure know a lot about Gujarat now. In the word grid below, help them find three monuments, three kings and three gods or goddesses.

```
W  T  H  S  O  M  N  A  T  H  A
A  K  S  H  A  R  D  H  A  M  S
D  S  U  R  Y  A  D  E  V  G  D
J  H  U  L  T  A  M  I  N  A  R
J  E  H  A  N  G  I  R  J  K  L
C  F  H  B  H  I  M  D  E  V  W
W  Q  A  S  H  O  K  A  W  E  S
S  H  I  V  A  D  F  B  Z  R  D
D  A  M  A  H  A  V  I  R  Y  G
```

Working hard

I want to live in Gujarat forever. But if I do, what kind of work will I have to do?

People in Gujarat are hard-working. They are known to be great businessmen. Let's see what people here do.

FARMER, FARMER, WHAT DO YOU GROW?

Because so much of Gujarat is desert land, agriculture is hard in these areas. But in the plains, farmers grow crops like jowar, rice, wheat and bajra. Farmers have to manage cropping patterns depending on weather. Cotton, tobacco and banana have become important. Thanks to the forests, bamboo, teak and different types of wood are also produced.

Banana fields

Teakwood forests

HERE COMES THE MILKMAN

The Gujarat dairies are very unique. Some years ago, farmers decided to form a co-operative. This was so successful that in a place called Anand, many farmers have set up large factories to process milk and milk products. Now these farmers are able to make and sell not just milk but ghee, butter, cream and buttermilk too! Mmmmm!

COTTON CRAFT

A lot of cotton is grown in Gujarat and then converted into cloth too! So there are many people who work in factories in the cotton industry.

Cotton yarn

Spot the Difference

Look at these two pictures of a farmer with his cattle. Can you spot eight differences in the two pictures?

BIG INDUSTRIES

Other very big industries in which thousands of people work are petrochemicals, chemicals, engineering, fertilizers and many more.

PETROLEUM PLENTY

Gujarat produces a lot of India's petroleum. This is because there are many, many refineries here that the government and lots of companies have set up. A lot of the oil and gas that we use for energy in India comes from Gujarat. So you can imagine how many people work in these refineries and oil rigs. A lot!

SPARKLING BRIGHT

Gujarat is one of the largest producers of processed diamonds in the whole world! Wow! There are thousands of factories in which people work hard, polishing, cutting and sorting diamonds.

Did you know?

Because of its long coastline, there are many fisheries here. And many ports too, from where goods are imported and exported.

HANDICRAFT HAPPINESS

The handicrafts of Gujarat are famous all over the world. For many generations, people worked in their traditional craft, like making furniture, embroidery, leather work, bandhani printing and weaving. Many younger people don't want to carry on the tradition. They would rather work in modern businesses. But the government is trying to encourage these people to carry on their family traditions so that this kind of wonderful handicraft work stays alive.

Gujarat's crafts are turned into wall-hangings, jackets, skirts and carpets. They are sold all over the world.

Fabulous FAN

Look at this amazing fan! Can you draw one like this and make a lovely pattern on it too?

Yum yum yum

At last, at last! My favourite part! What's the food like here, Daadu Dolma?

Ha! I already know. Gujarat has amazing dhoklas. Right, Daadu?

Right! But that's just one of the many, many, many amazing dishes you get here. Come, let's taste some of Gujarat's yummy food.

Papdi—a popular snack.

Khakras

VEGGIE DELIGHTS

Even though Gujarat has such a long coastline, a lot of Gujaratis are vegetarian and don't eat fish! This might be due to the impact of Jainism, since Jains are strict vegetarians. You get the most creative vegetarian food in Gujarat! And do you know what? The taste differs depending on which part of Gujarat the food is cooked in. Surat, Kutch, Kathiawad—all these regions have their own distinct taste.

SUPER SNACKS

Gujarati snacks are world famous. They are called farsans. Dhoklas are made of gram flour or rice flour. They are fluffy and light. People eat them with chutney. The famous faafda is yet another mouth-watering crisp snack that people love to eat along with crisp, sugary jalebis. Yummmmmm!

Faafda with jalebis

Dhokla

SO MANY TYPES OF BREADS!

You could call them breads or types of rotis. It is difficult to find a state that has as many types as Gujarat does. Theplas, dhebras, puris, bajri rotlo, pooda, khakras—each one special in its own way.

Methi theplas

Mmm . . . yummm!!

OOOOH UNDHIYU!!

This unbelievable dish is a winter speciality in Gujarat. As soon as winter sets in, people rush out to get the special vegetables you get only during the colder months. This wonderful dish is made by simmering those vegetables seasoned with different spices, coriander and coconut. Traditionally, people would put this in a mud pot and cook it on a flame for hours.

KHANDVI

This is a delicious dish that looks yummy too! To make this, gram paste is spread on a flat surface. It is tightly rolled and cut into pieces. It is a light and lovely dish.

HANDVO

This is a yummy pie that is made with a special flour. It is cooked on a pan until it is golden brown. People eat it hot with chutneys.

GUJARATI DAAL

This daal is different from any other in India. Its sweet, sour and spicy taste is unique, and people adore it. It also has peanuts in it to add crunch.

What a feast!!!

DAAL DHOKLI

This unusual dish is probably the only one where the breads (rotis) are dunked into daal and then cooked. It's a big, one pot meal. People simply LOVE this with a dollop of ghee on top.

Delicious daal dhokli topped with some ghee.

Yummy MAZE

Mishki is beyond excited. There's a huge thaali of Gujarati food waiting for her at the end of this maze. Help her get to it!

What to wear?

I am going to dress up in some really traditional Gujarati clothes, Daadu.

Well then, you had better be prepared for some elaborate stuff!

ALL DRESSED UP

The traditional attire for men is rather elaborate. They wear a short frock-coat called a kediyu or angarakhu. Underneath this jacket, they wear a shirt called a peharan or kafani. This is worn over the dhoti, the long cloth wrapped around the waist. They also wear a colourful turban called a phento. There are many ways in which you can tie this turban.

THE GUJARATI SARI

Women in Gujarat wear the sari in a different way. Their pallu (one end of the sari) is thrown over the shoulder from the back. See, doesn't it look different?

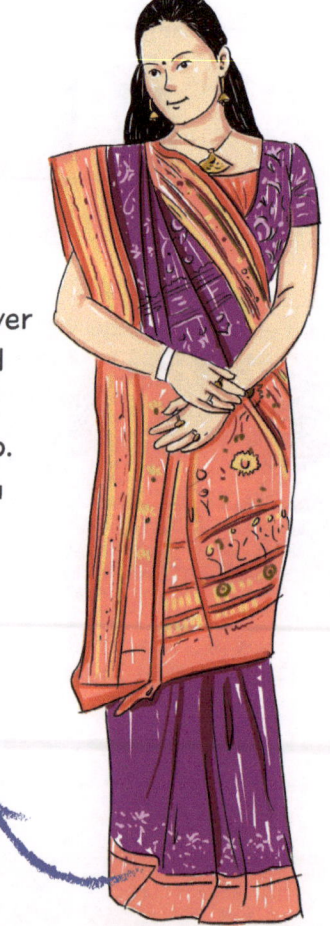

BANGLES AND JANGLES

In rural Gujarat, especially in the deserts of Kutch, women wear long, colourful skirts, blouses with lots of beautiful embroidery and mirror work, and a cloth called a dupatta thrown over their head. They wear lots of jewellery, like bangles that go all the way up their arms. They also wear seriously heavy neck pieces.

Gujarati style

Parsi style

THE PARSI TOUCH

We saw how Parsis have adopted Gujarati culture so beautifully. But there is a slight difference in the way they dress. Can you see it here?

MODERN TIMES

Though young men and women now wear Western clothes, slightly older folk still go with the traditional style of dressing.

CIRCLE COUNT

Mishki has made an animal shape using lots of bangles. Can you count how many bangles she has used?

Autograph, please?

I have my autograph book ready. Who are Gujarat's most famous people?

I hope you have a really thick book. Because there are a lot of really great men and women from Gujarat.

FATHER OF THE NATION

The most famous of them all—Mahatma Gandhi. The whole world knows him for his belief in non-violence.

SIR JAMSETJI TATA

He was a Parsi visionary, who founded the Tata empire and did a lot for people too!

SARDAR VALLABHBHAI PATEL

He was a great freedom fighter, who fought hard for India to remain united.

VIKRAM SARABHAI

He was a great scientist. He is known as the father of the Indian space programme.

NARI CONTRACTOR

This great cricketer played for India in many test matches.

NARENDRA MODI

Narendra Modi, the fourteenth prime minister of India, was once a simple tea seller. Imagine that!

SANJEEV KUMAR

Sanjeev Kumar was a well-known actor in Hindi and Gujarati films. His real name was Hari Jariwala.

DHIRUBHAI AMBANI

He was an industrialist who started the Reliance Group of companies, which is today famous all over the world.

BHUPEN KHAKHAR

He was an internationally renowned painter. Though he was born in Mumbai, he lived and worked in Vadodara.

MALLIKA SARABHAI

Mallika Sarabhai is a dancer, choreographer, writer and actor, who is also the daughter of scientist Vikram Sarabhai.

VINOO MANKAD

Vinoo Mankad is another great cricketer. His son Ashok Mankad also played for India.

CRACK THE CODE

Can you help Mishki and Pushka crack this code? The answer is something that Gandhiji believed in.

| P = 1 | E = 2 | A = 3 | C = 4 |
| F = 5 | O = 6 | R = 7 | L = 8 |

1	2	3	4	2		5	6	7		3	8	8

Once upon a time . . .

Daadu, are you going to tell us a nice story from Gujarat? I am sure there must be many.

Of course. Like so many other states, there are many traditional Gujarati stories that grandmothers tell their grandchildren. I will tell you one of these stories.

RUPALI BA'S BRAVERY

Many, many years ago, in the dry deserts of Kutch, people had to travel from one place to another only on camel carts. The desert was a dangerous place, with no villages for miles and miles. There were bands of robbers who would prey on unsuspecting travellers and rob them of everything they had.

To keep themselves safe from such robbers, people began to hire strong guards to accompany them on these dangerous journeys. Gema was one such guard.

Gema was big and strong. He had become famous as a man whom no thug could defeat. In fact, robbers were believed to be so scared of Gema, that they never came anywhere near a group travelling with Gema by their side.

Unfortunately, all this fame made Gema rather lazy. He became careless and too full of himself.

In Gema's village, there lived a pretty young woman called Rupali Ba. One day, Rupali Ba had to travel with her father-in-law, Bapuji, from one village to another. But the villages were far apart, and they had to travel through a vast desert.

They decided to take Gema with them. The next day, the entire group set out on a big camel cart. Rupali Ba was wearing a lot of jewellery, as women often did in that region. They rode for miles and miles. The sun was hot. Gema began to feel very sleepy. Before long, he was snoring loudly.

The camels trudged on through the hot desert. Rupali Ba and Bapuji were lulled to sleep by the slow and steady movement.

Mile after mile they went, as the sun rose higher and higher and soon began to set.

It became dark. There was no village in sight, so Bapuji decided they would stop for the night.

Suddenly, they heard the neighing of horses. They saw lights that were far away but were coming towards them. Bapuji tried to wake Gema, but Gema was fast asleep, snoring loudly.

Bapuji shook Gema hard. 'Wake up, you good-for-nothing fellow! Is this why we have brought you along?' But Gema snored on. Thunder and lightning would not have woken him up.

Suddenly, a big group of robbers attacked them. They were armed with daggers and flaming torches. They grabbed the sleeping Gema and tied him up. They were about to grab the jewellery off Rupali Ba, when she said, 'Wait! My father-in-law is old. I will give you the jewellery myself if you promise not to harm him.'

The robbers stopped in surprise. They were used to people trembling and begging for mercy. They had never encountered a woman who spoke to them so bravely.

They looked at each other. That was all Rupali Ba needed. As soon as they were distracted, she leapt out of the cart. She quickly untied Gema. She had hidden chilli powder in a box. She flung the chilli powder in their eyes. While they struggled to open their eyes, she grabbed a thick stick and attacked them fiercely. Blinded by the chilli powder, they were soon overcome by Rupali Ba.

With the help of Bapuji, she tied them up. Then, with a shamefaced Gema, the group travelled on. When they reached their destination, the story of Rupali Ba's bravery spread far and wide.

Even today, people in the deserts of Gujarat talk about the brave young woman, who managed to defeat robbers and keep her family safe.

TRAVEL DIARY

Have you enjoyed this trip to Gujarat with your friends Mishki and Pushka—and, of course, with Daadu Dolma?

Now you can make your own Gujarat diary. And if you ever visit Gujarat, make sure you take pictures and put them in the photo box.

The first place I would visit in Gujarat:

_____

If I had ever met Gandhiji, this is what I would have said to him:

_____

The one Gujarati dish I am definitely going to eat:

_____

The monument I think is the most interesting:

_____

The one famous person from Gujarat I would love to meet:

_____

The most exciting city in Gujarat is:

_____

The festival from Gujarat that I think is the most fun:

_____

The five words that I think describe Gujarat the best are:

_____

_____

_____

_____

My Gujarat memories:

ANSWERS

page 9 WORD SEARCH

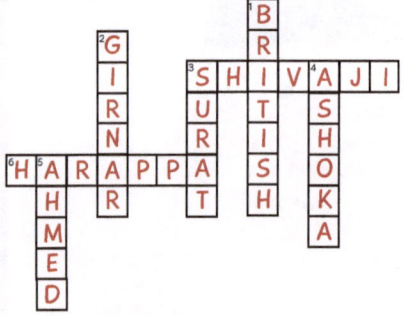

V I N D H Y A U I O
W S A T P U R A E W
D E A R A V A L L I
S A H Y A D R I R Y
C D R G I R N A R G
W S A R A S W A T I
N J F N A R M A D A
S A B A R M A T I B

page 11 WHAT'S ODD

Lion, Elephant, Himalaya, Ganga

page 13 SCRAMBLED UP

GANDHINAGAR, BARODA, DWARKA, AHMEDABAD, BHUJ, SURAT

page 17 CRAZY CROSSWORD

page 19 HIDDEN WORDS

Here are some words you can make:
art, ass, has, hat, hut, rat, rut, sat, tar, arts,
aura, hart, hats, hurt, huts, rash, rats, rush,
rust, shut, star, tars, thus, tsar, stash, trash

page 21 MATCH THE WORDS

What news?—Soo khabar?; I don't know—Maney
khabar nathi; I am fine—Hoon maja ma choo;
I am thirsty—Maney taras laagi che; How are
you?—Kem cho?; Bye-bye—Aav jo

page 25 POEM TIME

dance, around, along

page 29 PUSHKA'S KITE

Green kite

page 31 WORD LADDER

HOSE, POSE, POT

page 33 THAT'S ODD

Door, Wall, Window

page 39 WORD GRID

W T H S O M N A T H A
A K S H A R D H A M S
D S U R Y A D E V G D
J H U L T A M I N A R
J E H A N G I R J K L
C F H B H I M D E V W
W Q A S H O K A W E S
S H I V A D F B Z R D
D A M A H A V I R Y G

page 41 SPOT THE DIFFERENCE

page 47 YUMMY MAZE

page 49 CIRCLE COUNT

Eighteen circles

page 53 CRACK THE CODE

PEACE FOR ALL